Contents

Overview

In the online marketplace, consumers can transact business without the constraints of time or distance. One can log on to the Internet day or night and purchase almost anything one desires, and advances in mobile technology allow advertisers to reach consumers nearly anywhere they go. But cyberspace is not without boundaries, and deception is unlawful no matter what the medium. The FTC has enforced and will continue enforcing its consumer protection laws to ensure that products and services are described truthfully online, and that consumers understand what they are paying for. These activities benefit consumers as well as sellers, who expect and deserve the opportunity to compete in a marketplace free of deception and unfair practices.

The general principles of advertising law apply online, but new issues arise almost as fast as technology develops — most recently, new issues have arisen concerning space-constrained screens and social media platforms. This FTC staff guidance document describes the information businesses should consider as they develop ads for online media to ensure that they comply with the law. Briefly,

1. The same consumer protection laws that apply to commercial activities in other media apply online, including activities in the mobile marketplace. The FTC Act's prohibition on "unfair or deceptive acts or practices" encompasses online advertising, marketing, and sales. In addition, many Commission rules and guides are not limited to any particular medium used to disseminate claims or advertising, and therefore, apply to the wide spectrum of online activities.

2. When practical, advertisers should incorporate relevant limitations and qualifying information into the underlying claim, rather than having a separate disclosure qualifying the claim.

3. Required disclosures must be clear and conspicuous. In evaluating whether a disclosure is likely to be clear and conspicuous, advertisers should consider its placement in the ad and its proximity to the relevant claim. The closer the disclosure is to the claim to which it relates, the better. Additional considerations include: the prominence of the disclosure; whether it is unavoidable; whether other parts of the ad distract attention from the disclosure; whether the disclosure needs to be repeated at different places on a website; whether disclosures in audio messages are presented in an adequate volume and cadence; whether visual disclosures

appear for a sufficient duration; and whether the language of the disclosure is understandable to the intended audience.

4. To make a disclosure clear and conspicuous, advertisers should:

- Place the disclosure as close as possible to the triggering claim.

- Take account of the various devices and platforms consumers may use to view advertising and any corresponding disclosure. If an ad is viewable on a particular device or platform, any necessary disclosures should be sufficient to prevent the ad from being misleading when viewed on that device or platform.

- When a space-constrained ad requires a disclosure, incorporate the disclosure into the ad whenever possible. However, when it is not possible to make a disclosure in a space-constrained ad, it may, under some circumstances, be acceptable to make the disclosure clearly and conspicuously on the page to which the ad links.

- When using a hyperlink to lead to a disclosure,

  - make the link obvious;

  - label the hyperlink appropriately to convey the importance, nature, and relevance of the information it leads to;

  - use hyperlink styles consistently, so consumers know when a link is available;

  - place the hyperlink as close as possible to the relevant information it qualifies and make it noticeable;

  - take consumers directly to the disclosure on the click-through page;

  - assess the effectiveness of the hyperlink by monitoring click-through rates and other information about consumer use and make changes accordingly.

- Preferably, design advertisements so that "scrolling" is not necessary in order to find a disclosure. When scrolling is necessary, use text or visual cues to encourage consumers to scroll to view the disclosure.

- Keep abreast of empirical research about where consumers do and do not look on a screen.

- Recognize and respond to any technological limitations or unique characteristics of a communication method when making disclosures.

- Display disclosures before consumers make a decision to buy — e.g., before they "add to shopping cart." Also recognize that disclosures may have to be repeated before purchase to ensure that they are adequately presented to consumers.

- Repeat disclosures, as needed, on lengthy websites and in connection with repeated claims. Disclosures may also have to be repeated if consumers have multiple routes through a website.

- If a product or service promoted online is intended to be (or can be) purchased from "brick and mortar" stores or from online retailers other than the advertiser itself, then any disclosure necessary to prevent deception or unfair injury should be presented in the ad itself — that is, before consumers head to a store or some other online retailer.

- Necessary disclosures should not be relegated to "terms of use" and similar contractual agreements.

- Prominently display disclosures so they are noticeable to consumers, and evaluate the size, color, and graphic treatment of the disclosure in relation to other parts of the webpage.

- Review the entire ad to assess whether the disclosure is effective in light of other elements — text, graphics, hyperlinks, or sound — that might distract consumers' attention from the disclosure.

- Use audio disclosures when making audio claims, and present them in a volume and cadence so that consumers can hear and understand them.

- Display visual disclosures for a duration sufficient for consumers to notice, read, and understand them.

- Use plain language and syntax so that consumers understand the disclosures.

5. If a disclosure is necessary to prevent an advertisement from being deceptive, unfair, or otherwise violative of a Commission rule, and it is not possible to make the disclosure clearly and conspicuously, then that ad should not be disseminated. This means that if a particular platform does not provide an opportunity to make clear and conspicuous disclosures, then that platform should not be used to disseminate advertisements that require disclosures.

Negative consumer experiences can result in lost consumer goodwill and erode consumer confidence. Clear, conspicuous, and meaningful disclosures benefit advertisers and consumers.

I. Introduction

Day in and day out, businesses advertise and sell their products and services online.[1] The online universe presents a rewarding and fast-paced experience for consumers, but also raises interesting — and occasionally complex — questions about the applicability of laws that were developed long before "dot com," "smartphone," and "social media" became household terms.

In May 2000, following a public comment period and a public workshop held to discuss the applicability of FTC rules and guides to online activities, FTC staff issued Dot Com Disclosures. That guidance document examined how the Commission's consumer protection statutes, rules, and guides apply to online advertising and sales and discussed FTC requirements that disclosures be presented clearly and conspicuously, in the context of online advertising.

In May 2011, FTC staff began seeking input to modify and update the guidance document to reflect the dramatic changes in the online world in the preceding eleven years. After three public comment periods and a public workshop, this revised staff guidance document was issued in March 2013.[2]

This document provides FTC staff guidance concerning the making of clear and conspicuous online disclosures that are necessary pursuant to the laws the FTC enforces. It does not, however, purport to cover every issue associated with online advertising disclosures, nor is it intended to provide a safe harbor from potential liability. It is intended only to provide guidance concerning practices that may increase the likelihood that a disclosure is clear and conspicuous. Whether a particular ad is deceptive, unfair, or otherwise violative of a Commission rule will depend on the specific facts at hand. The ultimate test is not the size of the font or the location of the disclosure, although they are important considerations; the ultimate test is whether the information intended to be disclosed is actually conveyed to consumers.

---

1. In this document, the term "online" includes advertising and marketing via the Internet and other electronic networks. It is device neutral and encompasses advertising and marketing on mobile devices, such as smartphones and tablets.

2. This staff guidance document only addresses disclosures required pursuant to laws that the FTC enforces. It does not address disclosures that may be required pursuant to local, state (*e.g.*, many sweepstake requirements), or other federal laws or regulations (*e.g.*, regulations issued by the Consumer Financial Protection Bureau or the Food and Drug Administration).

There is no litmus test for determining whether a disclosure is clear and conspicuous, and in some instances, there may be more than one method that seems reasonable. In such cases, the best practice would be to select the method more likely to effectively communicate the information in question.

II. The Applicability of FTC Law to Online Advertising

The FTC Act's prohibition on "unfair or deceptive acts or practices" broadly covers advertising claims, marketing and promotional activities, and sales practices in general.[3] The Act is not limited to any particular medium. Accordingly, the Commission's role in protecting consumers from unfair or deceptive acts or practices encompasses advertising, marketing, and sales online, as well as the same activities in print, television, telephone, and radio. The Commission has brought countless law enforcement actions to stop fraud and deception online and works to educate businesses about their legal obligations and consumers about their rights.

For certain industries or subject areas, the Commission issues rules and guides. Rules prohibit specific acts or practices that the Commission has found to be unfair or deceptive.[4] Guides help businesses in their efforts to comply with the law by providing examples or direction on how to avoid unfair or deceptive acts or practices.[5] Many rules and guides address claims about products or services or advertising in general and apply to online

---

3. The Commission's authority covers virtually every sector of the economy, except for certain excluded industries, such as common carrier activities and the business of insurance, airlines, and banks.

4. The Commission issues rules pursuant to Section 5 of the FTC Act when it has reason to believe that certain unfair or deceptive acts or practices are prevalent in an industry. 15 U.S.C. § 57a(a)(1)(B). In addition, the Commission promulgates rules pursuant to specific statutes, which are designed to further particular policy goals.

5. Guides are "administrative interpretations of laws administered by the Commission." 16 C.F.R. § 1.5. Although guides do not have the force and effect of law, if a person or company fails to comply with a guide, the Commission might bring an enforcement action alleging an unfair or deceptive practice in violation of the FTC Act.

advertising, as well as to other media.[6] Therefore, the plain language of many rules and guides applies to claims made online.[7] For example, the Mail or Telephone Order Merchandise

---

6. The following rules and guides are included in this category: Guides for the Nursery Industry (16 C.F.R. Part 18); Guides for the Rebuilt, Reconditioned and Other Used Automobile Parts Industry (16 C.F.R. Part 20); Guides for the Jewelry, Precious Metals, and Pewter Industries (16 C.F.R. Part 23); Guides for Select Leather and Imitation Leather Products (16 C.F.R. Part 24); Guides Against Deceptive Pricing (16 C.F.R. Part 233); Guides Against Bait Advertising (16 C.F.R. Part 238); Guides for the Advertising of Warranties and Guarantees (16 C.F.R. Part 239); Guide Concerning Use of the Word "Free" and Similar Representations (16 C.F.R. Part 251); Guides for Private Vocational and Distance Education Schools (16 C.F.R. Part 254); Guides Concerning Use of Endorsements and Testimonials in Advertising (16 C.F.R. Part 255); Guides Concerning Fuel Economy Advertising for New Automobiles (16 C.F.R. Part 259); Guides for the Use of Environmental Marketing Claims (16 C.F.R. Part 260); Rules and Regulations Under the Wool Products Labeling Act of 1939 (16 C.F.R. Part 300); Rules and Regulations Under Fur Products Labeling Act (16 C.F.R. Part 301); Rules and Regulations Under the Textile Fiber Products Identification Act (16 C.F.R. Part 303); Energy and Water Use Labeling for Consumer Products under the Energy Policy and Conservation Act ("Energy Labeling Rule") (16 C.F.R. Part 305); Contacts Lens Rule (16 C.F.R. Part 315); Prohibition of Energy Market Manipulation Rule (16 C.F.R. Part 317); Deceptive Advertising as to Sizes of Viewable Pictures Shown by Television Receiving Sets (16 C.F.R. Part 410); Retail Food Store Advertising and Marketing Practices (16 C.F.R. Part 424); Use of Prenotification Negative Option Plans (16 C.F.R. Part 425); Power Output Claims for Amplifiers Utilized in Home Entertainment Products (16 C.F.R. Part 432); Preservation of Consumers' Claims and Defenses (16 C.F.R. Part 433); Mail or Telephone Order Merchandise (16 C.F.R. Part 435); Disclosure Requirements and Prohibitions Concerning Franchising (16 C.F.R. Part 436); Business Opportunity Rule (16 C.F.R. Part 437); Credit Practices (16 C.F.R. Part 444); Used Motor Vehicle Trade Regulation Rule (16 C.F.R. Part 455); Labeling and Advertising of Home Insulation (16 C.F.R. Part 460); Interpretations of Magnuson-Moss Warranty Act (16 C.F.R. Part 700); Disclosure of Written Consumer Product Warranty Terms and Conditions (16 C.F.R. Part 701); Pre-Sale Availability of Written Warranty Terms (16 C.F.R. Part 702); Informal Dispute Settlement Procedures (16 C.F.R. Part 703).

7. A rule or guide applies to online activities if its scope is not limited by how claims are communicated to consumers, how advertising is disseminated, or where commercial activities occur. The Commission has a program in place to systematically review its rules and guides to evaluate their continued need and to make any necessary changes. As needed, the Commission has and will continue to amend or clarify the scope of any particular rule or guide in more detail during its regularly scheduled review. For example, the Energy Labeling Rule was updated to clarify that "catalog" includes "material disseminated over the Internet" and to allow certain disclosures to be made available using the Internet. *See* 72 Fed. Reg. 49,948, 49,957, 49,961 (Aug. 29, 2007).

The first Dot Com Disclosures guidance document contained a section discussing how certain FTC rules and guides apply to online activities. Since that time, the Commission has addressed many of these issues in rulemakings or its periodic rule and guide reviews, and the information is widely understood given the ubiquitous nature and use of online technology. Nevertheless, the principles articulated in the original Dot Com Disclosures remain the same. For the most part, rules and guides that use terms such as "written," "writing," and "printed" apply online, and email may be used to comply with certain requirements to provide or send required notices or documents to consumers as long as consumers understand or expect to receive such information by email. For example, warranties communicated through visual text online are no different than paper versions and the same rules apply. The requirement to make warranties available at the point of purchase can be accomplished easily online by, for example, using a clearly-labeled hyperlink, in close proximity to the description of the warrantied product, such as "get warranty information here" to lead to the full text of the warranty, and presenting the warranty in a way that it can be preserved either by downloading or printing so consumers can refer to it after purchase. Disclosure of Written Consumer Product Warranty Terms and Conditions, 16 C.F.R. § 701.3 and Pre-Sale Availability of Written Warranty Terms, 16 C.F.R. § 702.3. Another example involves the Telemarketing Sales Rule. Advertisers who send email and text messages that invite consumers to telephone the sender in order to make a purchase are subject to the Telemarketing Sales Rule, unless they qualify for the direct mail exemption under 16 C.F.R. 310.6(b)(6) by clearly and conspicuously making certain specified disclosures in the original solicitation.

rule, which addresses the sale of merchandise that is ordered by mail, telephone, facsimile or computer, applies to those sales regardless of "the method used to solicit the order."[8] Solicitations made in print, on the telephone, radio, TV, or online naturally fall within the rule's scope. In addition, the Guides Concerning the Use of Endorsements and Testimonials in Advertising ("Endorsement Guides") apply to "any advertising message . . . that consumers are likely to believe reflects the opinions, beliefs, findings, or experience of a party other than the sponsoring advertiser . . . ."[9] The Guides refer to advertising without limiting the media in which it is disseminated and, therefore, encompass online ads.[10]

III. Clear and Conspicuous Disclosures in Online Advertisements

When it comes to online ads, the basic principles of advertising law apply:

1. Advertising must be truthful and not misleading;[11]

2. Advertisers must have evidence to back up their claims ("substantiation");[12] and

3. Advertisements cannot be unfair.[13]

---

8. 16 C.F.R. § 435.2(a).

9. 16 C.F.R. § 255.0(b).

10. Indeed, when the Endorsement Guides were reviewed in 2009, examples involving blogs were included, to make clear that the FTC Act applies to this then-new form of social media marketing.

11. As explained in the FTC's Deception Policy Statement, an ad is deceptive if it contains a statement — or omits information — that is likely to mislead consumers acting reasonably under the circumstances and is "material" or important to a consumer's decision to buy or use the product. *See FTC Policy Statement on Deception, appended to Cliffdale Associates, Inc.*, 103 F.T.C. 110, 174 ("Deception Policy Statement"), also available at www.ftc.gov/bcp/policystmt/ad-decept.htm. A statement also may be deceptive if the advertiser does not have a reasonable basis to support the claim. *See FTC Policy Statement on Advertising Substantiation, appended to Thompson Medical Co.*, 104 F.T.C. 648, 839 (1984), *aff'd*, 791 F.2d 189 (D.C. Cir. 1986), also available at www.ftc.gov/bcp/guides/ad3subst.htm.

12. Before disseminating an ad, advertisers must have appropriate support for all express and implied objective claims that the ad conveys to reasonable consumers. When an ad lends itself to more than one reasonable interpretation, there must be substantiation for each interpretation. The type of evidence needed to substantiate a claim may depend on the product, the claims, and what experts in the relevant field believe is necessary. If an ad specifies a certain level of support for a claim — "tests show x" — the advertiser must have at least that level of support.

13. According to the FTC Act, 15 U.S.C. § 45(n), and the FTC's Unfairness Policy Statement, an advertisement or business practice is unfair if it causes or is likely to cause substantial consumer injury that consumers could not reasonably avoid and that is not outweighed by the benefit to consumers or competition. *See FTC Policy Statement on Unfairness, appended to International Harvester Co.*, 104 F.T.C. 949, 1070 (1984), also available at www.ftc.gov/bcp/policystmt/ad-unfair.htm.

Unique features in online ads — including advertising delivered via social media platforms or on mobile devices — may affect how an ad and any required disclosures are evaluated.

A.   Background on Disclosures

Advertisers are responsible for ensuring that all express and implied claims that an ad conveys to reasonable consumers are truthful and substantiated. When identifying these claims, advertisers should not focus only on individual phrases or statements, but should consider the ad as a whole, including the text, product name, and depictions.[14] If an ad makes express or implied claims that are likely to be misleading without certain qualifying information, the information must be disclosed.

A disclosure can only qualify or limit a claim to avoid a misleading impression. It cannot cure a false claim. If a disclosure provides information that contradicts a material claim, the disclosure will not be sufficient to prevent the ad from being deceptive. In that situation, the claim itself must be modified.

Many Commission rules and guides spell out the information that must be disclosed in connection with certain claims. In many cases, these disclosures prevent a claim from being misleading or deceptive.[15] Other rules and guides require disclosures to ensure that consumers receive material information to assist them in making better-informed decisions,[16] or to implement statutes furthering public policy goals.[17] In all of these instances, if a disclosure is required, it must be clear and conspicuous.

---

14. Copy tests or other evidence of how consumers actually interpret an ad can be valuable. In many cases, however, the implications of the ad are clear enough to determine the existence of the claim by examining the ad alone, without extrinsic evidence.

15. For example, if an endorsement is not representative of the performance that consumers can generally expect to achieve with a product, advertisers must disclose the generally expected performance in the depicted circumstances. Endorsement Guides, 16 C.F.R. § 255.2.

16. For example, any solicitation for the purchase of consumer products with a warranty must disclose the text of the warranty offer or how consumers can obtain it for free. Pre-Sale Availability of Written Warranty Terms, 16 C.F.R. § 702.3.

17. For example, the required energy disclosures in the Energy Labeling Rule, 16 C.F.R. § 305, further the public policy goal of promoting energy conservation by providing consumers with clear comparative information.

B.   The Clear and Conspicuous Requirement

Disclosures that are required to prevent an advertisement from being deceptive, unfair, or otherwise violative of a Commission rule, must be presented "clearly and conspicuously."[18] Whether a disclosure meets this standard is measured by its performance — that is, how consumers actually perceive and understand the disclosure within the context of the entire ad. The key is the overall net impression of the ad — that is, whether the claims consumers take from the ad are truthful and substantiated.[19] If a disclosure is not seen or comprehended, it will not change the net impression consumers take from the ad and therefore cannot qualify the claim to avoid a misleading impression.

In reviewing their ads, advertisers should adopt the perspective of a reasonable consumer.[20] They also should assume that consumers don't read an entire website or online screen, just as they don't read every word on a printed page.[21] Disclosures should be placed as close as possible to the claim they qualify. Advertisers should keep in mind that having to scroll increases the risk that consumers will miss a disclosure.

In addition, it is important for advertisers to draw attention to the disclosure. Consumers may not be looking for — or expecting to find — disclosures. Advertisers are responsible for ensuring that their messages are truthful and not deceptive. Accordingly, disclosures must be communicated effectively so that consumers are likely to notice and understand them in connection with the representations that the disclosures modify. Simply making the disclosure available somewhere in the ad, where some consumers might find it, does not meet the clear and conspicuous standard.

If a disclosure is necessary to prevent an advertisement from being deceptive, unfair, or otherwise violative of a Commission rule, and if it is not possible to make the disclosure clear and conspicuous, then either the claim should be modified so the disclosure is not necessary or the ad should not be disseminated. Moreover, if a particular platform does not provide an

---

18. Some rules and guides, as well as some FTC cases, use the phrase "clearly and prominently" instead of "clearly and conspicuously." As used in FTC rules, guides, and cases, these two phrases are synonymous. They may have different meanings under other statutes.

19. Deception Policy Statement at 175-76.

20. Deception Policy Statement at 178. The Deception Policy Statement also says that "[w]hen representations or sales practices are targeted to a specific audience, such as children, the elderly, or the terminally ill, the Commission determines the effect of the practice on a reasonable member of that group." *Id.* at 179 (footnote omitted).

21. Deception Policy Statement at 180-81.

opportunity to make clear and conspicuous disclosures, it should not be used to disseminate advertisements that require such disclosures.[22]

C. What Are Clear and Conspicuous Disclosures?

There is no set formula for a clear and conspicuous disclosure; it depends on the information that must be provided and the nature of the advertisement. Some disclosures are quite short, while others are more detailed. Some ads use only text, while others use graphics, video, or audio, or combinations thereof. Advertisers have the flexibility to be creative in designing their ads, as long as necessary information is communicated effectively and the overall message conveyed to consumers is not misleading.

To evaluate whether a particular disclosure is clear and conspicuous, consider:

- the placement of the disclosure in the advertisement and its proximity to the claim it is qualifying;
- the prominence of the disclosure;
- whether the disclosure is unavoidable;
- the extent to which items in other parts of the advertisement might distract attention from the disclosure;
- whether the disclosure needs to be repeated several times in order to be effectively communicated, or because consumers may enter the site at different locations or travel through the site on paths that cause them to miss the disclosure;
- whether disclosures in audio messages are presented in an adequate volume and cadence and visual disclosures appear for a sufficient duration; and
- whether the language of the disclosure is understandable to the intended audience.

If there are indications that a significant proportion of reasonable consumers are not noticing or comprehending a necessary disclosure, the disclosure should be improved.

The following discussion uses these traditional factors to evaluate whether disclosures are likely to be clear and conspicuous in the context of online ads. Hyperlinks labeled as

---

22. This approach mirrors one articulated by the Commission in 1970, when it said that if disclosures in television ads could not be understood, then ads containing representations requiring those disclosures should not be aired. *See Commission Enforcement Policy Statement in Regard to Clear and Conspicuous Disclosures in Television Advertising* (Oct. 21, 1970).

Examples in the text link to mock ads in the appendix. Each mock ad presents a scenario to illustrate one or more particular factors. Advertisers must consider all of the factors, however, and evaluate an actual disclosure in the context of the ad as a whole.

1. Proximity and Placement

A disclosure is more effective if it is placed near the claim it qualifies or other relevant information. Proximity increases the likelihood that consumers will see the disclosure and relate it to the relevant claim or product. For print ads, an advertiser might measure proximity in terms of whether the disclosure is placed adjacent to the claim, or whether it is separated from the claim by text or graphics. The same approach can be used for online ads. Websites, and mobile applications, however, are interactive and have a certain depth — with multiple pages or screens linked together and pop-up screens, for example — that may affect how proximity is evaluated. Mobile devices also present additional issues because a disclosure that would appear on the same screen of a standard desktop computer might, instead, require significant vertical and horizontal scrolling on a mobile screen. In evaluating placement, advertisers should also take into consideration empirical research about where consumers do and do not look on a screen.

a. Evaluating Proximity

A disclosure is more likely to be effective if consumers view the disclosure and the claim that raises the need for disclosure (often referred to as a "triggering claim") together on the same screen. Example 1 Even if a disclosure is not tied to a particular word or phrase, it is more likely that consumers will notice it if it is placed next to the information, product, or service to which it relates.

Often, disclosures consist of a word or phrase that may be easily incorporated into the text, along with the claim. Doing so increases the likelihood that consumers will see the disclosure and relate it to the relevant claim.

In some circumstances, it may be difficult to ensure that a disclosure appears on the "same screen" as a claim or product information. Some disclosures are long and thus difficult to place next to the claims they qualify. In addition, computers, tablets, smartphones, and other connected devices have varying screen sizes that display ads and websites differently. In these situations, an advertiser might place a disclosure where consumers might have to scroll to reach it. Requiring consumers to scroll in order to view a disclosure may be problematic, however, because consumers who don't scroll enough (and in the right direction) may miss important qualifying information and be misled.

When advertisers are putting disclosures in a place where consumers might have to scroll in order to view them, they should use text or visual cues to encourage consumers to scroll and avoid formats that discourage scrolling.

Text prompts can indicate that more information is available. An explicit instruction like "see below for important information on restocking fees" will alert consumers to scroll and look for the information. The text prompt should be tied to the disclosure to which it refers. General or vague statements, such as "details below," provide no indication about the subject matter or importance of the information that consumers will find and are not adequate cues.

The visual design of the page also could help alert consumers to the availability of more information. For example, text that clearly continues below the screen, whether spread over an entire page or in a column, would indicate that the reader needs to scroll for additional information. Advertisers should consider how the page is displayed when viewed on different devices.

Scroll bars along the edges of a screen are not a sufficiently effective visual cue. Although the scroll bars may indicate to some consumers that they have not reached the bottom or sides of a page, many consumers may not look at the scroll bar and some consumers access the Internet with devices that don't display a scroll bar.

The design of some pages might indicate that there is no more information following and, therefore, no need to continue scrolling. If the text ends before the bottom of the screen or readers see an expanse of blank space, they may stop scrolling and miss the disclosure. Example 2 They will also likely stop scrolling when they see the information and types of links that normally signify the bottom of a webpage, e.g., "contact us," "terms and conditions," "privacy policy," and "copyright." In addition, if there is a lot of unrelated information — either words or graphics — separating a claim and a disclosure, even a consumer who is prompted to scroll might miss the disclosure or not relate it to a distant claim they've already read.

If scrolling is necessary to view a disclosure, then, ideally, the disclosure should be unavoidable — consumers should not be able to proceed further with a transaction, e.g., click forward, without scrolling through the disclosure. Making a disclosure unavoidable increases the likelihood that consumers will see it.

Because of their small screens, smartphones (and some tablets) potentially require horizontal, as well as vertical, scrolling. Placing a disclosure in a different column of a webpage from the claim it modifies could make it unlikely that consumers who have to zoom in to read the claim on a small screen will scroll right or left to a different column and read the disclosure. Example 3 Optimizing a website for mobile devices will eliminate the need for consumers to scroll right or left, although it will not necessarily address the need for vertical scrolling.

b. Hyperlinking to a Disclosure

Hyperlinks allow additional information to be placed on a webpage entirely separate from the relevant claim. Hyperlinks can provide a useful means to access disclosures that are not integral to the triggering claim, provided certain conditions (discussed below) are met. Hyperlinked disclosures may be particularly useful if the disclosure is lengthy or if it needs to be repeated (because of multiple triggering claims, for example).

However, in many situations, hyperlinks are not necessary to convey disclosures. If a disclosure consists of a word or phrase that may be easily incorporated into the text, along with the claim, this placement increases the likelihood that consumers will see the disclosure and relate it to the relevant claim.

Disclosures that are an integral part of a claim or inseparable from it should not be communicated through a hyperlink. Instead, they should be placed on the same page and immediately next to the claim, and be sufficiently prominent so that the claim and the disclosure are read at the same time, without referring the consumer somewhere else to obtain this important information. This is particularly true for cost information or certain health and safety disclosures. Example 4 Indeed, required disclosures about serious health and safety issues are unlikely to be effective when accessible only through a hyperlink. Similarly, if a product's basic cost (*e.g.*, the cost of the item before taxes, shipping and handling, and any other fees are added on) is advertised on one page, but there are significant additional fees the consumer would not expect to incur in order to purchase the product or use it on an ongoing basis, the existence and nature of those additional fees should be disclosed on the same page and immediately adjacent to the cost claim, and with appropriate prominence.

However, if the details about the additional fees are too complex to describe adjacent to the price claim, those details may be provided by using a hyperlink. Example 5 The hyperlink should be clearly labeled to communicate the specific nature of the information to which it leads, *e.g.*, "Service plan required. <u>Get service plan prices</u>." The hyperlink should appear adjacent to the price. Moreover, because consumers should not have to click on hyperlinks to understand the full amount they will pay, all cost information — including any such additional fees — should be presented to them clearly and conspicuously prior to purchase.

The key considerations for evaluating the effectiveness of all hyperlinks are:

- the labeling or description of the hyperlink;

- consistency in the use of hyperlink styles;

- the placement and prominence of the hyperlink on the webpage or screen; and

- the handling of the disclosure on the click-through page or screen.

Choosing the right label for the hyperlink. A hyperlink that leads to a disclosure should be labeled clearly and conspicuously. The hyperlink's label — the text or graphic assigned to it — affects whether consumers actually click on it and see and read the disclosure.

- **Make it obvious.** Consumers should be able to tell that they can click on a hyperlink to get more information. Simply underlining text may be insufficient to inform consumers that the text is a hyperlink. Using multiple methods of identifying hyperlinks, such as both a different color from other text and underscoring, makes it more likely that hyperlinks will be recognized.

- **Label the link to convey the importance, nature, and relevance of the information to which it leads.** <u>Example 6</u> The hyperlink should give consumers a reason to click on it. That is, the label should make clear that the link is related to a particular advertising claim or product and indicate the nature of the information to be found by clicking on it. The hyperlink label should use clear, understandable text. Although the label itself does not need to contain the complete disclosure, it may be necessary to incorporate part of the disclosure to indicate the type and importance of the information to which the link leads. On the other hand, in those cases where seeing a hyperlinked disclosure is unavoidable if a consumer is going to take any action with respect to a product or service — *e.g.*, the product or service can only be purchased online and the consumer must click on that link to proceed to a transaction — the label of the hyperlink may be less important.

- **Don't hide the ball.** Some text links provide no indication about why a claim is qualified or the nature of the disclosure. <u>Example 7</u> In many cases, simply hyperlinking a single word or phrase in the text of an ad is not likely to be effective. Although some consumers may understand that additional information is available, they may have different ideas about the nature of the information and its significance.

Hyperlinks that simply say "disclaimer," "more information," "details," "terms and conditions," or "fine print" do not convey the importance, nature, and relevance of the information to which they lead and are likely to be inadequate. Even labels such as "important information" or "important limitations" may be inadequate. Examples 8 & 9 Unfortunately, there is no one-size-fits-all word or phrase that can be used as a hyperlink label, but more specificity will generally be better.

- **Don't be subtle.** Symbols or icons by themselves are not likely to be effective as hyperlink labels leading to disclosures that are necessary to prevent deception.[23] Example 10 A symbol or icon might not provide sufficient clues about why a claim is qualified or the nature of the disclosure.[24] It is possible that consumers may view a symbol as just another graphic on the page. Even if a website explains that a particular symbol or icon is a hyperlink to important information, consumers might miss the explanation, depending on where they enter the site and how they navigate through it.

- **Account for technological differences and limitations.** Consider whether and how your linking technique will work on the various programs and devices that could be used to view your advertisement.[25]

Using hyperlink styles consistently increases the likelihood that consumers will know when a link is available. Although the text or graphics used to signal a hyperlink may differ across websites and applications, treating hyperlinks inconsistently within a single site or application can increase the chances that consumers will miss — or not click on — a

---

23. The Commission has, however, acknowledged the potential utility of icons in the privacy area. *See* FTC, *Protecting Consumer Privacy in an Era of Rapid Change, Recommendations for Businesses and Policymakers* (Mar. 2012), *available at* www.ftc.gov/os/2012/03/120326privacyreport.pdf; *see also* FTC Staff, *Mobile Apps for Kids: Current Privacy Disclosures are Disappointing* (Feb. 2012), *available at* www.ftc.gov/os/2012/02/120216mobile_apps_kids.pdf.

24. Symbols and icons also are used in different ways online, which could confuse consumers as to where the related disclosure can be found. Some online symbols and icons are hyperlinks that click through to a separate page; some are meant to communicate disclosure information themselves; and others are static, referring to a disclosure at the bottom of the page.

25. For example, "mouse-overs" may not work on mobile devices that have no cursor to hover over a link.

disclosure hyperlink. For example, if hyperlinks usually are underlined in a site, chances are consumers wouldn't recognize italicized text as being a link, and could miss the disclosure.

Placing the link near relevant information and making it noticeable. The hyperlink should be proximate to the claim that triggers the disclosure so consumers can notice it easily and relate it to the claim. Examples 11 & 12 Typically, this means that the hyperlink is adjacent to the triggering term or other relevant information. Consumers may miss disclosure hyperlinks that are separated from the relevant claim by text, graphics, blank space, or intervening hyperlinks, especially on devices with small screens. Format, color, or other graphics treatment also can help to ensure that consumers notice the link. (See below for more information on prominence.)

Getting to the disclosure on the click-through should be easy. The click-through page or screen — that is, the page or screen the hyperlink leads to — must contain the complete disclosure and that disclosure must be displayed prominently. Distracting visual factors, extraneous information, and opportunities to "click" elsewhere before viewing the disclosure can obscure an otherwise adequate disclaimer.

- **Get consumers to the message quickly.** The hyperlink should take consumers directly to the disclosure. They shouldn't have to search a click-through page or go to other places for the information. In addition, the disclosure should be easy to understand.

- **Pay attention to indicia that hyperlinked disclosures are not effective.** Although advertisers are not required to use them, some available tools may indicate to advertisers that their disclosures accessed through hyperlinks are not effective. For example, advertisers can monitor click-through rates, *i.e.*, how often consumers click on a hyperlink and view the click-through information. Advertisers also can evaluate the amount of time visitors spend on a certain page, which may indicate whether consumers are reading the disclosure.

- **Don't ignore your data.** If hyperlinks are not followed, another method of conveying the required information would be necessary.

c. Using High Tech Methods for Proximity and Placement

Disclosures may be displayed on websites or in applications in many ways. For example, a disclosure may be placed in a frame that remains constant even as the consumer scrolls down the page or navigates through another part of the site or application. A disclosure also might be displayed in a window that pops up or on interstitial pages that appear while another webpage is loading. New techniques for displaying information are being developed all the time. But there are special considerations for evaluating whether a technique is appropriate for providing required disclosures.

- **Don't ignore technological limitations.** Some browsers or devices may not support certain techniques for displaying disclosures or may display them in a manner that makes them difficult to read. For example, a disclosure that requires Adobe Flash Player will not be displayed on certain mobile devices.

- **Don't use blockable pop-up disclosures.** Advertisers should not disclose necessary information through the use of pop-ups that could be prevented from appearing by pop-up blocking software.

- **Be aware of other issues with pop-up disclosures.** Even the use of unblockable pop-ups to disclose necessary information may be problematic. Some consumers may not read information in pop-up windows or interstitials because they immediately close the pop-ups or move to the next page in pursuit of completing their intended tasks, or because they don't associate information in a pop-up window or on an interstitial page to a claim or product they haven't encountered yet. However, advertisers can take steps to avoid such problems, *e.g.*, by requiring the consumer to take some affirmative action to proceed past the pop-up or interstitial (for example, by requiring consumers to choose between "yes" and "no" buttons without use of preselected buttons before continuing). Research may be useful to help advertisers determine whether a particular technique is an effective method of communicating information to consumers.

d. Displaying Disclosures Prior to Purchase

Disclosures must be effectively communicated to consumers before they make a purchase or incur a financial obligation. In general, disclosures are more likely to be effective if they are provided in the context of the ad, when the consumer is considering the purchase. Different considerations apply, however, in different situations. Where advertising and selling are combined on a website or mobile application — that is, the consumer will be completing the transaction online — disclosures should be provided before the consumer makes the decision to buy, *e.g.*, before clicking on an "order now" button or a link that says "add to shopping cart." Example 13

- **Don't focus only on the order screen.** Some disclosures must be made in conjunction with the relevant claim or product. Consumers may not relate a disclosure on the order screen to information they viewed much earlier. It also is possible that after surfing a company's website, some consumers may decide to purchase the product from the company's brick and mortar store. Those consumers would miss any disclosures placed only on the ordering screen. So that these consumers do not miss a necessary disclosure, it may have to be on the same page as the claim it qualifies.

When a product advertised online can be purchased from brick and mortar stores or from online retailers other than the advertiser itself, necessary disclosures should be made in the ad before consumers go to other outlets to make their purchase. Example 14 An in-store disclosure or one placed on an unrelated online retailer's website is unlikely to cure an otherwise deceptive advertisement.

e. Evaluating Proximity in Space-Constrained Ads

Many space-constrained ads displayed today are teasers. Because of their small size and/or short length, space-constrained ads, such as banner ads and tweets, generally do not provide very much information about a product or service. Often, consumers must click through to the website to get more information and learn the terms of an offer. If a space-constrained ad contains a claim that requires qualification, the advertiser disseminating it is not exempt from disclosure requirements.

- **Disclose required information in the space-constrained ad itself or clearly and conspicuously on the website to which it links.** In some cases, a required disclosure can easily be incorporated into a space-constrained ad. Example 15 In other instances, the disclosures may be too detailed to be disclosed effectively in the ad itself. These disclosures may sometimes be communicated effectively to consumers if they are made clearly and conspicuously on the website to which the ad links. In determining whether the disclosure should be placed in the space-constrained ad itself or on the website to which the ad links, advertisers should consider how important the information is to prevent deception, how much information needs to be disclosed, the burden of disclosing it in the ad itself, how much information the consumer may absorb from the ad, and how effective the disclosure would be if it were made on the website. If a product promoted in a space-constrained ad can be bought in a brick and mortar store, consumers who do not click through to a linked website would miss any disclosure that was not in the space-constrained ad itself. If the disclosure needs to be in the ad itself but it does not fit, the ad should be modified so it does not require such a disclosure or, if that is not possible, that space-constrained ad should not be used.

- **Use creativity to incorporate or flag required information.** Scrolling text or rotating panels in a banner ad can present an abbreviated version of a required disclosure that indicates additional important information and a more complete disclosure are available on the click-through page.

- **Use disclosures in each ad.** If a disclosure is required in a space-constrained ad, such as a tweet, the disclosure should be in each and every ad that would require a disclosure if that ad were viewed in isolation. Do not assume that consumers will see and associate multiple space-constrained advertisements. Example 16

- **Short-form disclosures might or might not adequately inform consumers of the essence of a required disclosure.** For example, "Ad:" at the beginning of a tweet or similar short-form message should inform consumers that the message is an advertisement, and the word "Sponsored" likely informs consumers that the message was sponsored by an advertiser. Other abbreviations or icons may or may not be adequate, depending on whether they are presented clearly and conspicuously, and whether consumers understand their meaning so they are not misled.[26] Example 17 Misleading a significant minority of reasonable consumers is a violation of the FTC Act.[27]

- **Maintaining disclosures with republication.** Advertisers should employ best practices to make it less likely that disclosures will be deleted from space-constrained ads when they are republished by others. Some disclosures can be placed at the beginning of a short-form message. Alternatively, if a disclosure is placed at the end of a message, the original message can be written with enough free space that the disclosure is not lost if the message is republished with a comment by others.

---

26. Empirical evidence may be necessary to demonstrate that certain abbreviations or icons are effective, at least until such time that their usage is sufficiently widespread to provide confidence that consumers see them and understand what they mean. As of the date of publication of this document, such evidence was not available.

27. Deception Policy Statement at 177 n.20.

- **Disclosures on the click-through.** In some instances — *e.g.*, when a teaser ad does not actually identify the product being advertised, so the consumer must click through to learn its identity, or when the advertised product is sold only through the advertiser's own website and the consumer must click through in order to take any action — a space-constrained ad can direct consumers to a website for more information if a detailed disclosure is necessary but will not fit in the space-constrained ad. The full disclosure must then be clearly and conspicuously displayed on the website.

- **Providing required disclosures in interactive ads.** If consumers can purchase a product within an interactive ad, all required disclosures should be included in the ad itself.

2. Prominence

It is the advertiser's responsibility to draw attention to the required disclosures.

Display disclosures prominently so they are noticeable to consumers. The size, color, and graphics of the disclosure affect its prominence.

- **Size Matters.** Disclosures that are at least as large as the claim to which they relate are more likely to be effective.

- **Color Counts.** A disclosure in a color that contrasts with the background emphasizes the text of the disclosure and makes it more noticeable. Information in a color that blends in with the background of the ad is likely to be missed. Example 18

- **Graphics Help.** Although using graphics to display a disclosure is not required, they may make the disclosure more prominent.

Evaluate the size, color, and graphics of the disclosure in relation to other parts of the website, email or text message, or application.[28] The size of a disclosure should be compared to the type size of the claim and other text on the screen. If a claim uses a particular color or graphic treatment, the disclosure can be formatted the same way to help ensure that consumers who see the claim are also able to see the disclosure and relate it back to the claim

---

28. Websites may display differently, depending on the program and device used. Advertisers should consider different display options to ensure that qualifying information is displayed clearly and conspicuously. Evaluating the prominence of the disclosure in relation to the rest of the ad, as it may appear on various devices, helps ensure that consumers are able to view the disclosure.

it modifies. In addition, the graphic treatment of the disclosure may be evaluated in relation to how graphics are used to convey other items in the ad.

Account for viewing on different devices. Most webpages viewable on desktop devices may also be viewable on smartphones. Therefore, unless a website defaults to a mobile-optimized (or similarly responsive) version,[29] advertisers should design the website so that any necessary disclosures are clear and conspicuous, regardless of the device on which they are displayed. Example 19 Among many other considerations, if a disclosure is too small to read on a mobile device and the text of the disclosure cannot be enlarged, it is not a clear and conspicuous disclosure. If a disclosure is presented in a long line of text that does not wrap around and fit on a screen, it is unlikely to be adequate.

Don't bury it. The prominence of the disclosure also may be affected by other factors. A disclosure that is buried in a long paragraph of unrelated text will not be effective. The unrelated text detracts from the message and makes it unlikely that a consumer would notice the disclosure or recognize its importance. Even though the unrelated information may be useful, advertisers must ensure that the disclosure is communicated effectively. For example, it is highly unlikely that consumers will read disclosures buried in "terms of use" and similar lengthy agreements. Even if such agreements may be sufficient for contractual or other purposes, disclosures that are necessary to prevent deception or unfairness should not be relegated to them. Similarly, simply because consumers click that they "agree" to a term or condition, does not make the disclosure clear and conspicuous.

A disclosure that addresses a subject other than the primary subject of the ad. Consumers who are trying to complete a task and obtain a specific product or service may not pay adequate attention to a disclosure that does not relate to the task at hand. This can be problematic if, for example, an advertiser is selling a product or service together with a negative option trial for a different product or service. In these circumstances, even a relatively prominent disclosure about the negative option trial could be missed by consumers because this additional product or service is not their primary focus. One way to increase the likelihood that consumers have actually read and understood a disclosure in such circumstances is to require consumers to affirmatively acknowledge having seen the disclosure by choosing between multiple answer options, none of which is preselected. Any such affirmative

---

29. Website operators can identify visitors who are using mobile devices to visit their websites and display a version of the site that has been designed or "optimized" to enable those consumers to view the site more easily.

acknowledgement should be displayed early in the decision-making process, *e.g.*, before the primary item is actually added to a shopping cart. Example 20

3. Distracting Factors in Ads

The clear and conspicuous analysis does not focus only on the disclosure itself. It also is important to consider the entire ad. Elements like graphics, sound, text, links that lead to other screens or sites, or "add to cart" buttons may result in consumers not noticing, reading, or listening to the disclosure. Example 21

- **Don't let other parts of an ad get in the way.** On television, moving visuals behind a text message make the text hard to read and may distract consumers' attention from the message. Using graphics online raises similar concerns: flashing images or animated graphics may reduce the prominence of a disclosure. Graphics on a webpage alone may not undermine the effectiveness of a disclosure. It is important, however, to consider all the elements in the ad, not just the text of the disclosure. Example 22

4. Repetition

It may be necessary to disclose information more than once to convey a non-deceptive message. Repeating a disclosure makes it more likely that a consumer will notice and understand it, and will also increase the likelihood that it will be seen by consumers who may be entering the website at different points. Still, the disclosure need not be repeated so often that consumers would ignore it or it would clutter the ad.

- **Repeat disclosures on lengthy sites and applications, as needed.** Consumers can access and navigate websites or applications in different ways. Many consumers may access a site through its home page, but others might enter in the middle, perhaps by linking to that page from a search engine or another website. Consumers also might not click on every page of the site and might not choose to scroll to the bottom of each page. And many may not read every word on every page of a website. As a result, advertisers should consider whether consumers who see only a portion of their ad are likely to be misled because they will either miss a necessary disclosure or not understand its relationship to the claim it modifies.

- **Repeat disclosures with repeated claims, as needed.** If claims requiring qualification are repeated throughout an ad, it may be necessary to repeat the disclosure, too. In some situations, the disclosure itself is so integral to the claim that it must always accompany the claim to prevent deception. In other instances, a clearly-labeled hyperlink could be repeated on each page where the claim appears, so that the full disclosure would be placed on only one page of the site.

5. Multimedia Messages and Campaigns

Online ads may contain or consist of audio messages, videos, animated segments, or augmented reality experiences (interactive computer-generated experiences) with claims that require qualification. As with radio and television ads, the disclosure should accompany the claim. In evaluating whether disclosures in these multimedia portions of online ads are clear and conspicuous, advertisers should evaluate all of the factors discussed in this guidance document, as well as these special considerations:

- **For audio claims, use audio disclosures.** The disclosure should be in a volume and cadence sufficient for a reasonable consumer to hear and understand it. The volume of the disclosure can be evaluated in relation to the rest of the message, and in particular, the claim. Of course, consumers who do not have speakers, appropriate software, or devices with audio capabilities or who have their sound turned off will not hear either the claim or the disclosure.

- **For written claims, use written disclosures.** Disclosures triggered by a claim or other information in an ad's written text should be made in writing, and not be placed solely in an audio or video clip. Consumers who do not have speakers, appropriate software, or devices with audio capabilities or who have their sound turned off will not hear an audio disclosure; similarly, consumers might not be able to view a video clip on some devices or simply might not choose to watch it.

- **Display visual disclosures for a sufficient duration.** Visual disclosures presented in video clips or other dynamic portions of online ads should appear for a duration sufficient for consumers to notice, read, and understand them. As with brief video superscripts in television ads, fleeting online disclosures are not likely to be effective.

Advertisers should also recognize that consumers today may be viewing their messages through multiple media (*e.g.*, watching television, surfing the web on a computer, viewing space constrained messages on a smartphone, etc.). This multiple media access does not alter the requirement that required disclosures be made clearly and conspicuously in each advertisement that would require a disclosure if viewed in isolation.

6. Understandable Language

For disclosures to be effective, consumers must be able to understand them. Advertisers should use clear language and syntax and avoid legalese or technical jargon. Disclosures should be as simple and straightforward as possible. Icons and abbreviations are not adequate to prevent a claim from being misleading if a significant minority of consumers do not understand their meaning.[30] Incorporating extraneous material into the disclosure also may diminish communication of the message to consumers.

IV. Conclusion

Although online commerce (including mobile and social media marketing) is booming, deception can dampen consumer confidence in the online marketplace. To ensure that products and services are described truthfully online and that consumers get what they pay for, the FTC will continue to enforce its consumer protection laws. Most of the general principles of advertising law apply to online ads, but new issues arise almost as fast as technology develops. The FTC will continue to evaluate online advertising, using traditional criteria, while recognizing the challenges that may be presented by future innovation. Businesses, as well, should consider these criteria when developing online ads and ensuring they comply with the law.

---

30. *See supra* note 23.

Appendix:
Examples

Example 1

The disclosure "imitation" needs to accompany the triggering term "pearl," so that consumers are not misled about the type of pearls being sold. The disclosure would not be as effective if it was separated from the word "pearl" or placed on a different page. The FTC's Guides for the Jewelry, Precious Metals, and Pewter Industries, 16 C.F.R. § 23.19, recognize this and advise that the disclosure "imitation" immediately precede the word pearl. In this situation, there is no reason to evaluate proximity differently in online ads than other types of ads.

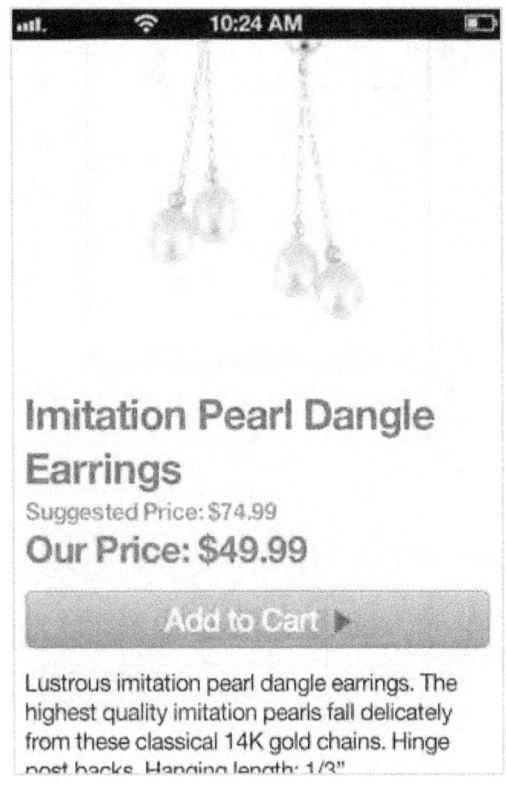

Example 2

This ad must disclose that the diamond weights are not exact and that a 3/4 carat diamond may weigh between .72 and .78 carats. Here, though, because of the blank space between the textual description of the product and the disclosure, even consumers who scroll down to the end of the text (see second screen) will probably think that there is no more information to view and are likely to miss the disclosure.

Example 3

Advertisers should take into consideration the variety of devices and platforms that consumers can use to view their ads and ensure that necessary disclosures are clear and conspicuous on any device or platform that is capable of displaying their message.

In this example, consumers might not expect a monthly service fee for cameras used to monitor their homes over the Internet, so a disclosure is necessary to prevent the ad from being misleading. Placing the disclosure in a different column than the camera price it qualifies, as in this example, rather than directly under the price information, makes it less likely that consumers viewing this webpage on a desktop computer would notice the disclosure here.

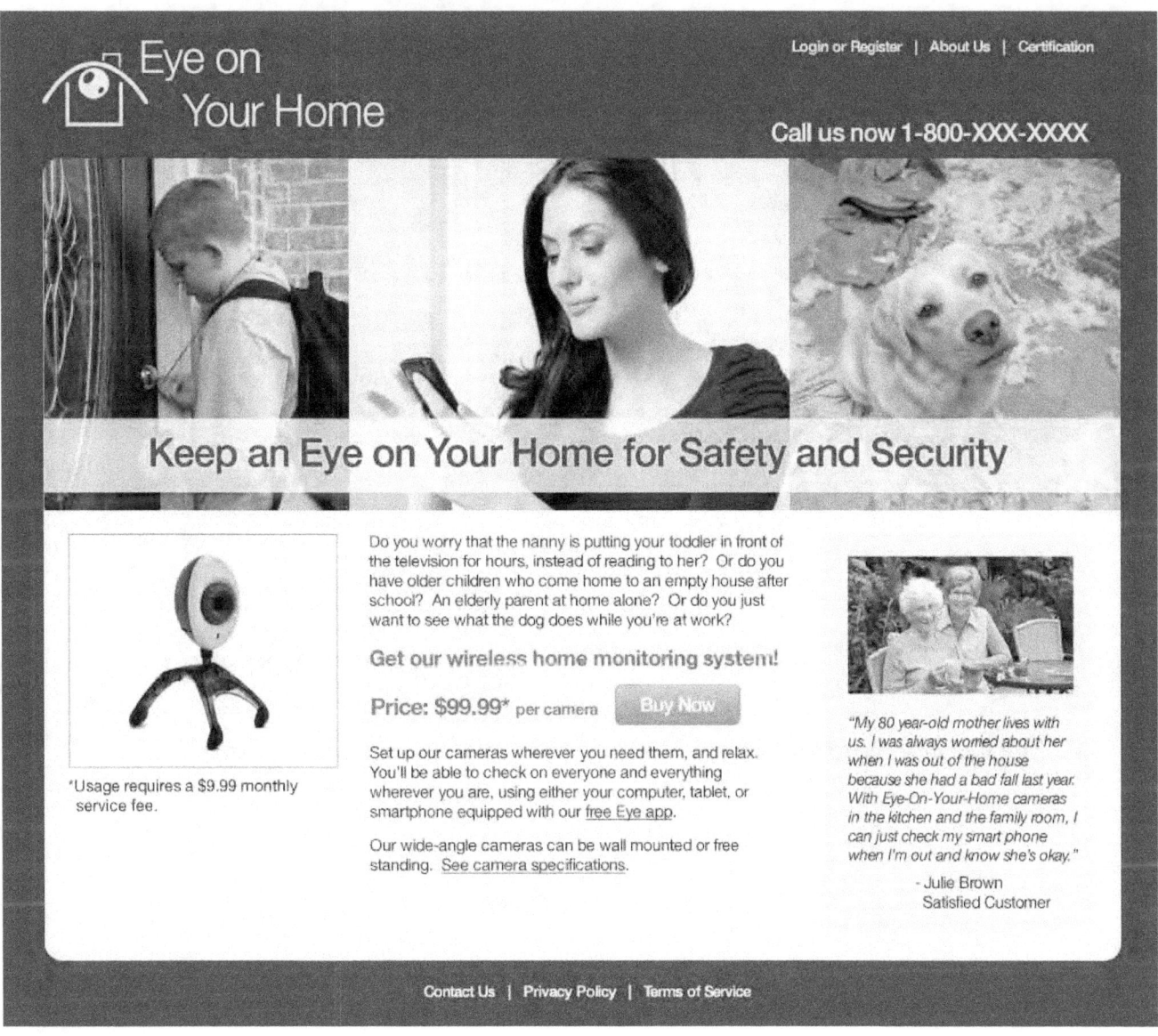

Webpage on a desktop

(continued on next page)

Example 3 (cont'd)

Consumers viewing this webpage on a smartphone or other device with a small screen, however, would likely find it too small to read (see mobile screen without zooming, below), requiring them to zoom in on the part or parts that they wish to read.

They are likely to zoom in on the center column (see zoomed-in mobile screen, below), which contains the main information on the page and might not scroll left to see the disclosure in the left column. As a result, consumers who use a smart phone to view this website, which has not been optimized for mobile devices, might easily miss the monthly monitoring fee disclosure.

Mobile screen (no zooming)

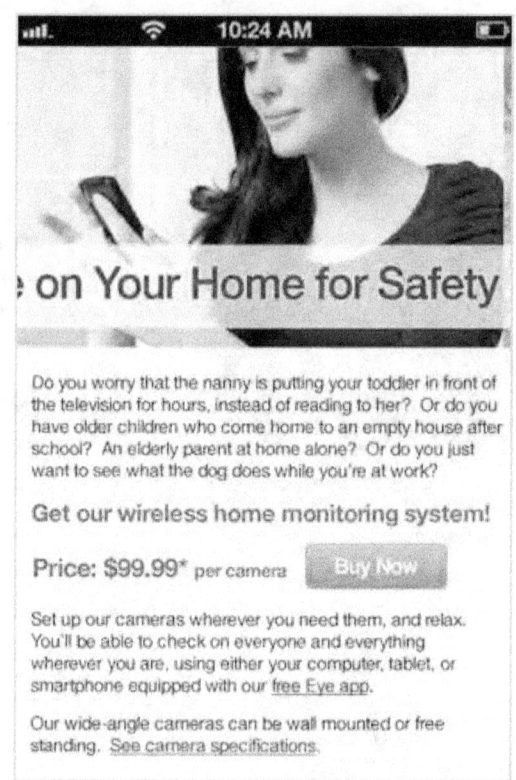

Mobile screen (zoomed-in)

Example 4

Hyperlinks should not be used to communicate disclosures that are an integral part of a claim or inseparable from it, including important health and safety information. In this example, the hyperlink "Important Health Information" leads to a disclosure, "Frost-a-tron may not keep perishable food items cold enough to prevent the growth of bacteria when the temperature is over 80°F, such as in a hot car. Use in these conditions could lead to food-borne illness." The fact that the cooler might not keep food cold enough to prevent the growth of dangerous bacteria should not be hidden behind a hyperlink, even one labeled "Important Health Information." This is especially true when the cooler is promoted for keeping perishable food fresh and cold on road trips. Moreover, any disclosure that is integral to the primary claim should be immediately adjacent to that claim.

Example 5

Although hyperlinks generally should not be used to disclose information integral to the claim — such as the existence and nature of additional fees consumers might not expect — a hyperlink can be used to disclose the details if they are too complex to describe next to the basic price information. Here the hyperlink leads to the disclosure, "Monitoring plan price: $15.95 per month with one camera, $9.95 per month/per camera with two cameras, $7.95 per month/per camera with three or more cameras. Save 10% with a 12-month commitment, 20% with a 24-month commitment. Additional 5% discount for seniors and families of active duty military personnel."

This information about the monitoring plan's prices is likely is too complex to appear adjacent to the price per camera claim, and thus can be placed behind a properly labeled hyperlink. The statement "Service plan required" and the hyperlink are next to the price per camera; and together, the statement and the hyperlink's label communicate to consumers the specific nature and importance of the information to which the hyperlink leads.

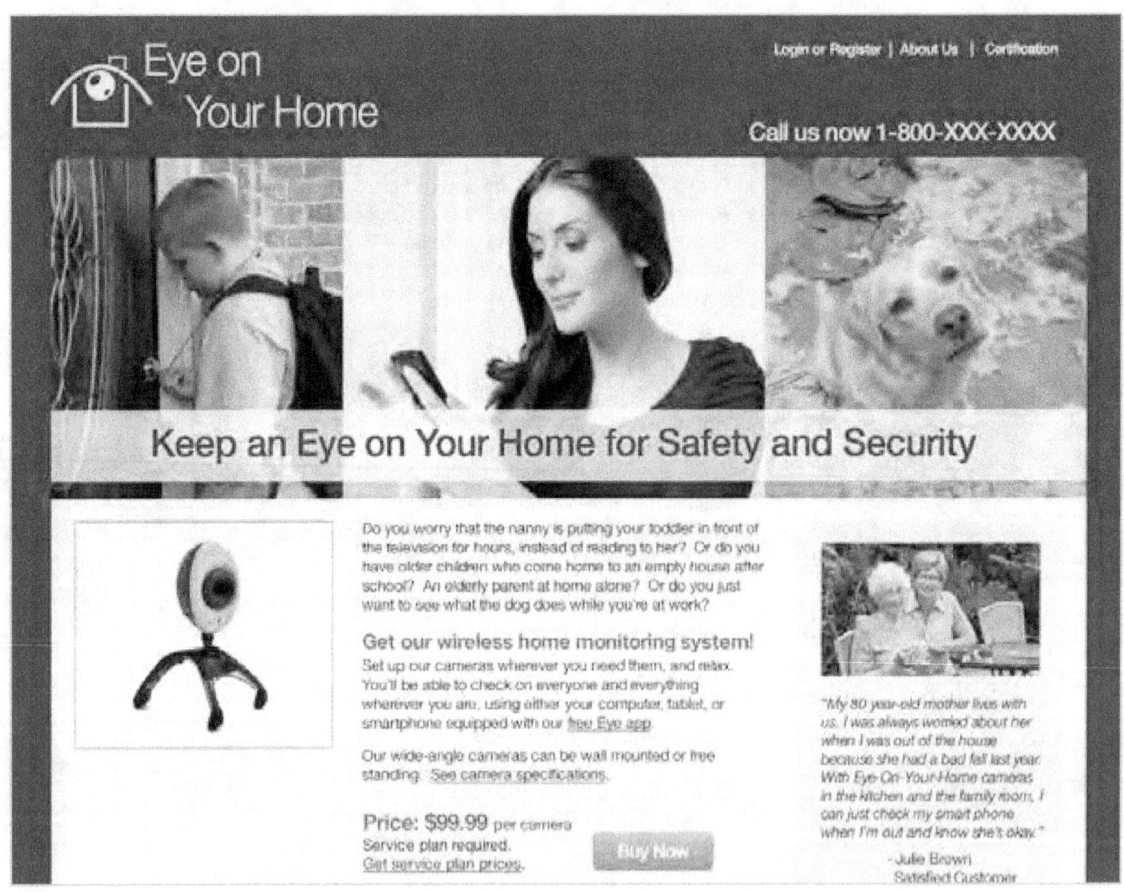

Moreover, all cost information, including any such fees, should be presented clearly and conspicuously to consumers prior to purchase.

Example 6

Because the advertiser's assertion that "Satisfaction is guaranteed" implies that dissatisfied consumers can get a full refund of the purchase price, the advertiser should clearly and conspicuously disclose any restocking fees.

The hyperlink "Restocking fee applies to all returns." leads to the disclosure, "If you return the Frost-a-tron within 30 days there is a restocking fee of $19.95. After 30 days and before 90 days, the restocking fee is $29.95. After 90 days, the restocking fee is $49.95. Shipping and handling fees are non-refundable. No COD on returns." The details in this return policy are likely too complex to disclose next to the guarantee. The label of the hyperlink adequately conveys the nature and relevance of the information to which it leads.

Example 7

This ad must disclose that the diamond weights are not exact and that a 3/4 carat diamond may weigh between .72 and .78 carats. Even if the hyperlink "3/4 Ct." clicks through to a page that lists the weight range for every size diamond sold by the advertiser, this disclosure is not clear and conspicuous.

Underlining "3/4 Ct." may or may not indicate to consumers that this is a hyperlink. Even if consumers recognize it as a hyperlink, the label here does not communicate the relevance of the information to which that link leads — in this case, to a disclosure that diamond weights are not exact, that the diamonds sold by this merchant may vary in weight, and that the advertised ¾ carat diamonds might each actually weight less than 0.75 carats. Consumers might expect to find additional general information about "carats" or diamond weights generally, but not necessarily information that qualifies the claim that they are purchasing diamonds of a specific weight.

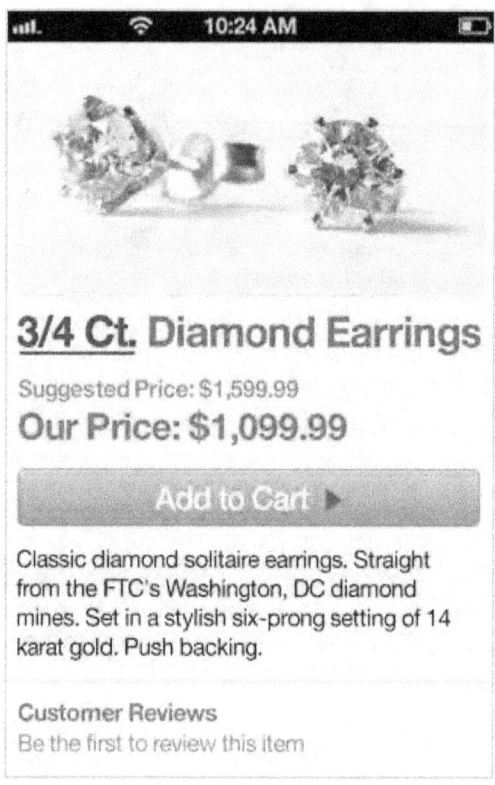

Example 8

Because the advertiser's assertion that "Satisfaction is guaranteed" implies that dissatisfied consumers can get a full refund of the purchase price, the advertiser should disclose any restocking fees. The hyperlink "Disclaimer" leads to the disclosure, "If you return the Frost-a-tron within 30 days there is a restocking fee of $19.95. After 30 days and before 90 days, the restocking fee is $29.95. After 90 days, the restocking fee is $49.95. Shipping and handling fees are non-refundable. No COD on returns."

The hyperlink label "Disclaimer" does not adequately convey that the information to which this hyperlink leads concerns significant restocking fees applied to all product returns; nor would hyperlinks labeled "Disclosure," "Details," or even "Return Information."

In contrast, the hyperlink in Example 6, "Restocking fee applies to all returns," does convey the nature and importance of the information in question.

Example 9

This ad must disclose that the diamond weights are not exact and that a 3/4 carat diamond may weigh between .72 and .78 carats. Even if the hyperlink clicks through to a page that lists the weight range for every size diamond sold by the advertiser, this disclosure is not clear and conspicuous because the hyperlink's label does not indicate the importance of the information to which the link leads so that consumers understand why they should click on it. Although the label does indicate that more information about the earrings is available if the consumer clicks through, it does not indicate that it is related to the weight of the diamonds being advertised. Consumers could expect, for example, that this link takes them to shipping and ordering information, rather than information about the diamond weights.

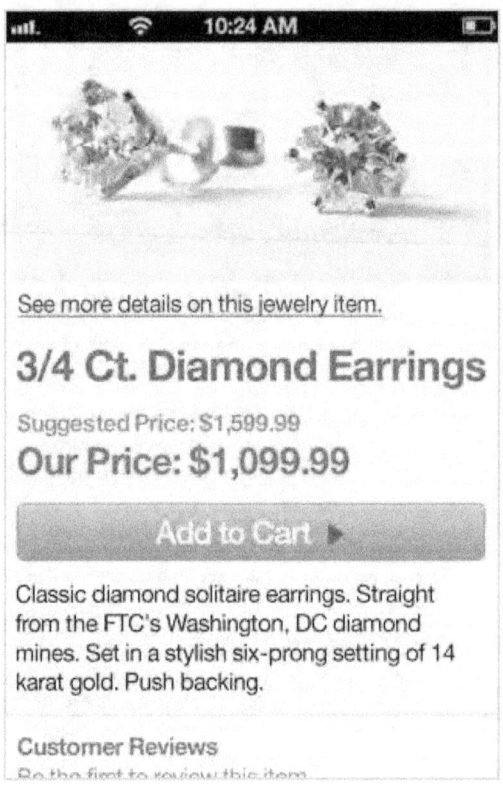

Example 10

Julie Brown's endorsement is followed by a symbol consisting of the letters "FS" in a circle that is intended to disclose that she received a free sample (in this case, a free camera) in exchange for providing her endorsement.

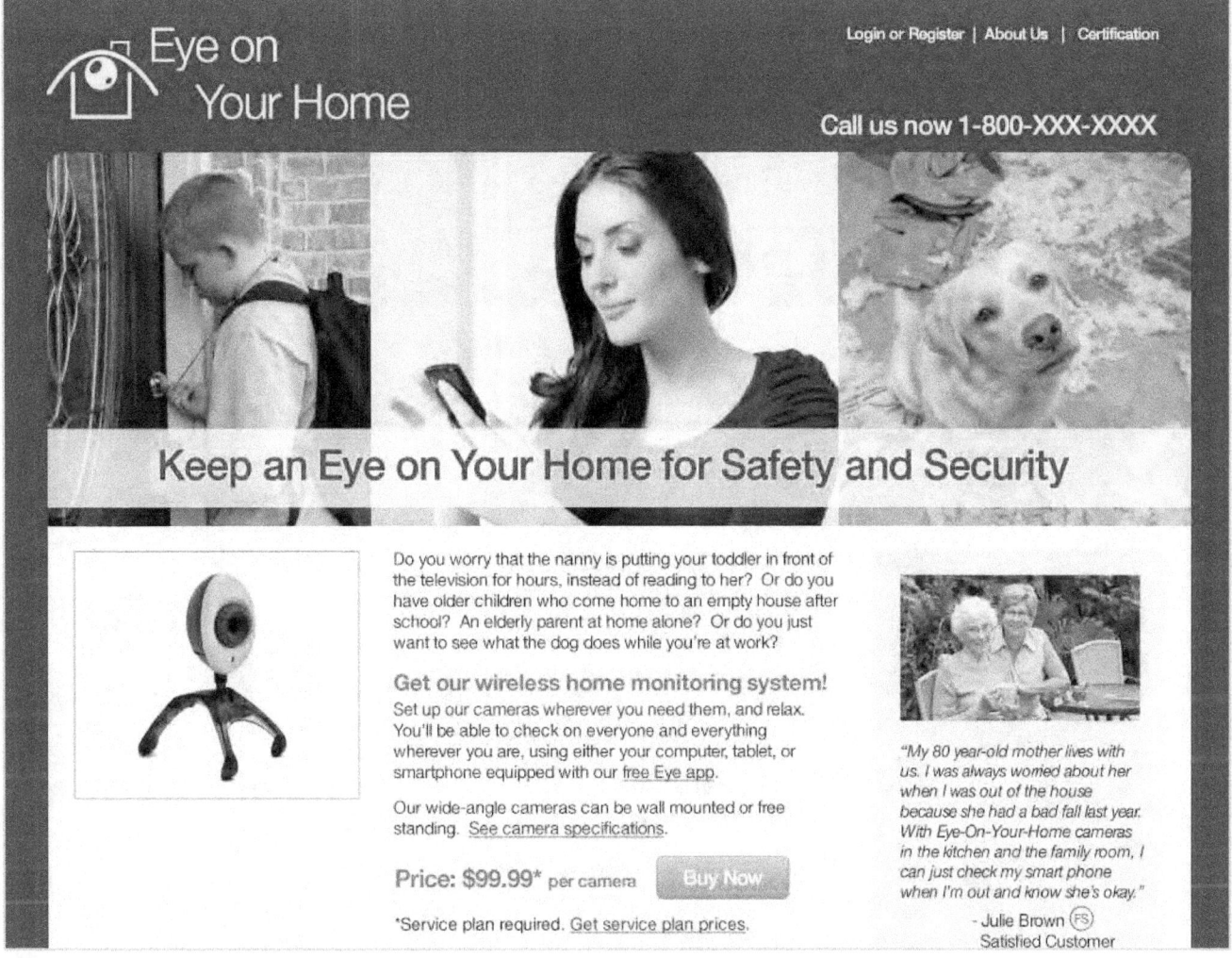

Icons, abbreviations, and symbols such as this are not adequate to prevent a claim from being misleading if they do not provide sufficient clues about why a claim is qualified or about the nature of the disclosure, or if consumers simply do not understand their meaning. The fact that the icon or symbol also functions as a hyperlink to an explanation of its meaning would not be sufficient to make the disclosure clear and conspicuous.

Example 11

Hyperlinks should be adjacent to the claims to which they relate, in order to increase the likelihood that consumers will see them and understand their relevance.

In this example, the hyperlink about restocking fees is right next to the claim that triggers the need for this qualifying information — that satisfaction is guaranteed.

Example 12

Hyperlinks should be adjacent to the claim to which they relate, in order to increase the likelihood that consumers will see them and understand their relevance.

In this example, the substantial gap between the end of the webpage's main text and the hyperlink makes it unlikely that consumers will notice the hyperlink. In addition, as noted in Example 9, the hyperlink is inadequately labeled.

Example 13

If the purchase or use of the advertised product entails significant additional charges beyond the basic price of the product and consumers reasonably might not expect those charges, they should be disclosed prominently on the same page as, and immediately adjacent to, statements of the product's basic cost.

In this example, disclosure of the existence and amount of a monthly monitoring fee only on the check-out page (see next page) would likely be deemed insufficiently clear and conspicuous; this fee should be clearly stated next to the price of the cameras on the preceding website pages that provide that price information.

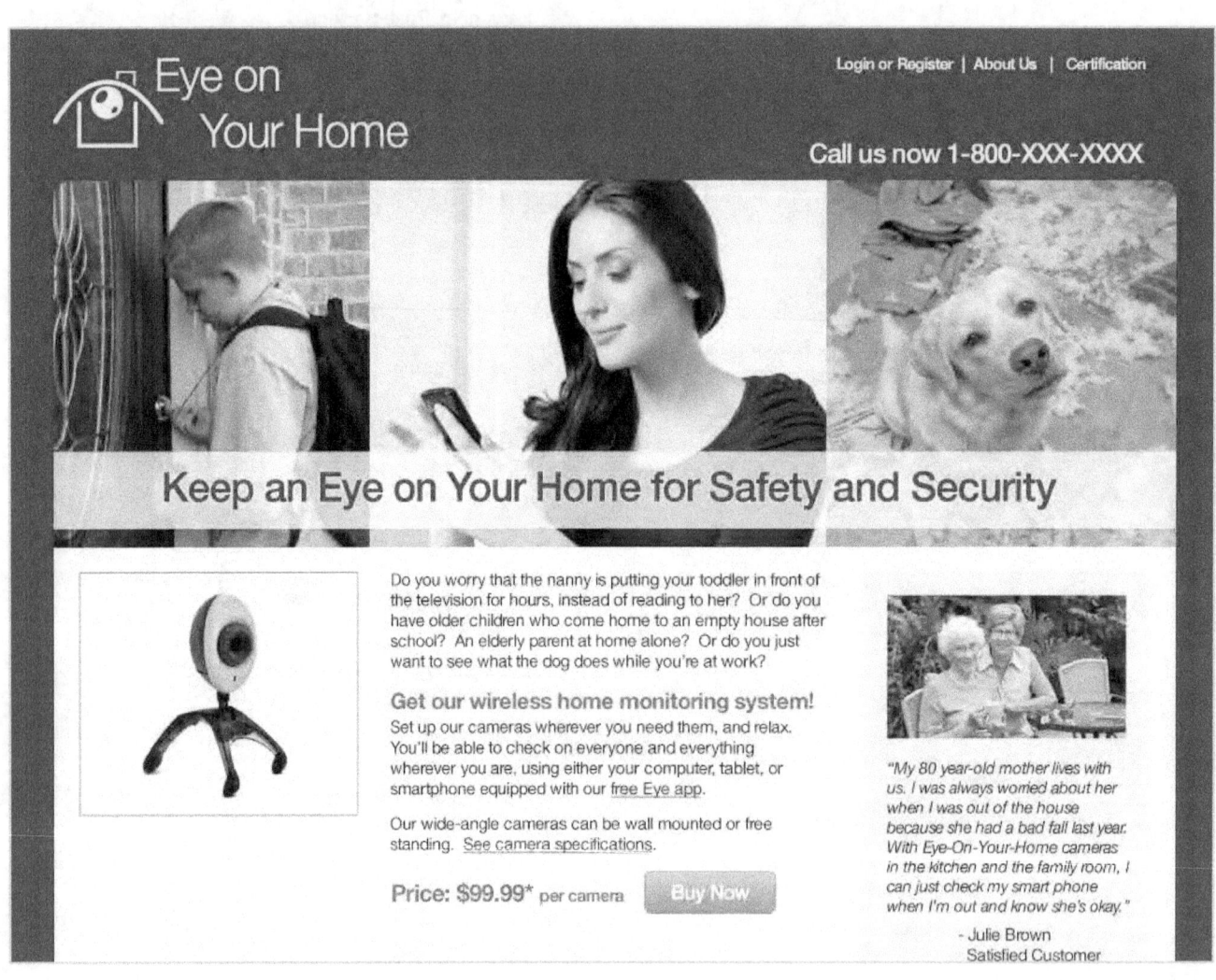

(continue on next page)

Example 13 (continued)

However, disclosure on the check-out page of the sales tax the consumer owes on this purchase, as well as reasonable shipping and handling charges, would not be problematic, because consumers expect these charges.

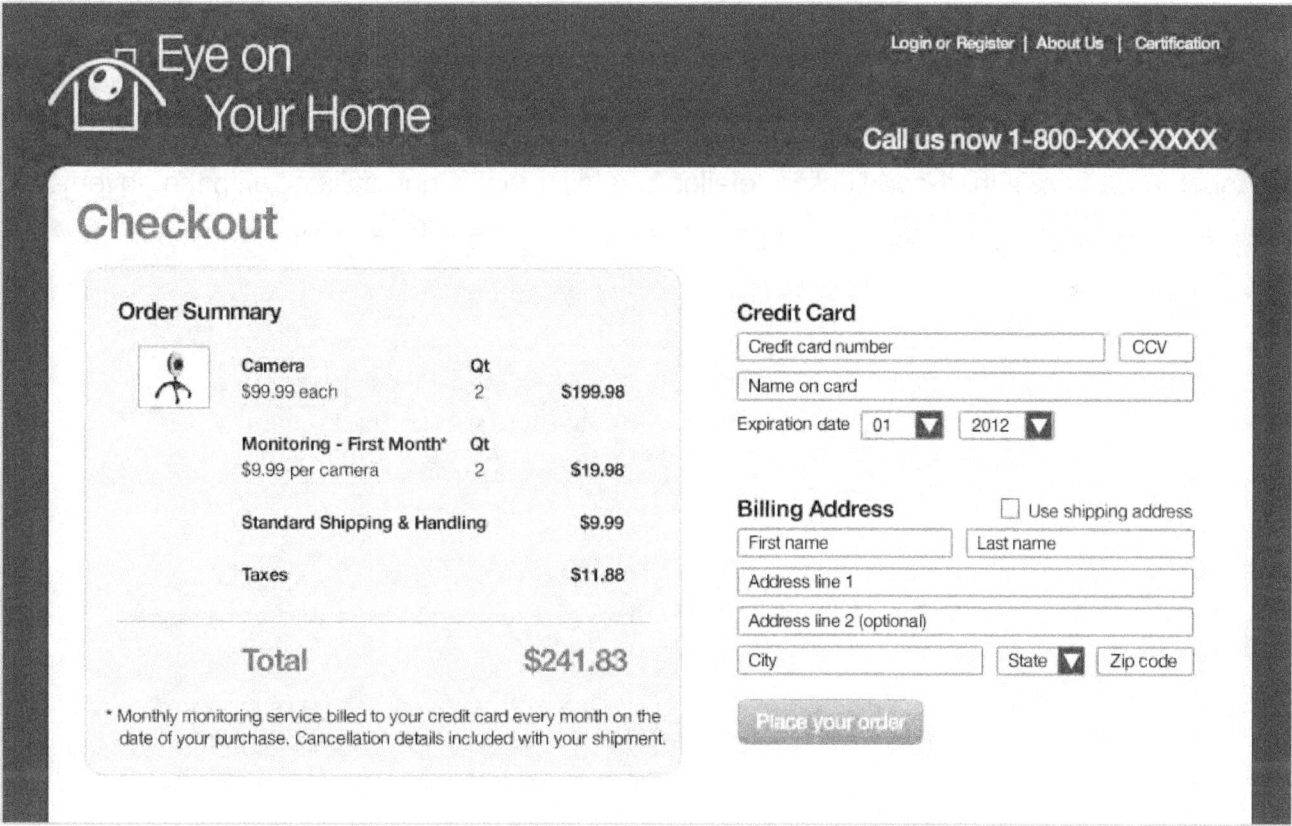

Example 14

This space-constrained message requires two disclosures: (1) that JuliStarz is a paid endorser for Fat-away; and (2) the amount of weight that consumers who use Fat-away can generally expect to lose in the depicted circumstances, which is much less than the 30 pounds Juli says she lost in 6 weeks. See Guides Concerning the Use of Endorsements and Testimonials in Advertising, 16 CFR Part 255.

Even if the link in the message led directly to those disclosures on the Fat-away website, those disclosures would not be adequate if consumers could purchase Fat-away at a brick and mortar store or from a third-party online retailer (a retailer that is not affiliated with the advertiser). In either case, they might not click through to the Fat-away website, and thus would not see these disclosures.

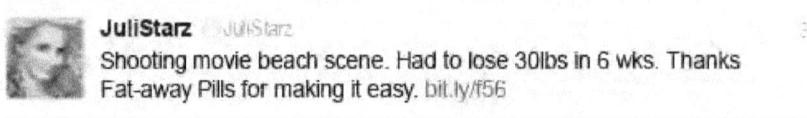

Example 15

   In some cases, required disclosures can easily be incorporated into a space-constrained ad. This space-constrained message requires two disclosures: (1) that JuliStarz is a paid endorser for Fat-away; and (2) the amount of weight that consumers who use Fat-away can generally expect to lose in the depicted circumstances, which is much less than the 30 pounds Juli says she lost in 6 weeks. This space-constrained ad signals that Juli is a paid endorser by beginning with "Ad:" which only takes up four characters. It also succinctly discloses, "Typical loss: 1lb/wk."

JuliStarz JuliStarz   3h
Ad: Shooting movie beach scene. Had to lose 30lbs in 6 wks. Thanks Fat-away Pills for making it easy. Typical loss: 1lb/wk.

Example 16

The initial space-constrained message requires two disclosures: (1) that Juli is a paid endorser for Fat-away; and (2) the amount of weight that consumers who use Fat-away can generally expect to lose in the depicted circumstances, which is much less than the 30 pounds Juli says she lost in 6 weeks. Putting that information in a subsequent message is problematic, because unrelated messages may arrive in the interim. By the time Juli's disclosures arrive, consumers might no longer be reading these messages, or they simply might not realize that those disclosures pertain to the original message.

Example 17

These space-constrained messages all require the following disclosures: (1) that JuliStarz is a paid endorser for Fat-away; and (2) the amount of weight that consumers who use Fat-away can generally expect to lose in the depicted circumstances which is much less than the 30 pounds Juli says she lost in 6 weeks. Although each of these messages includes an abbreviation or link that leads to disclosure of the relevant information, each of them may be inadequate to prevent consumers from being misled.

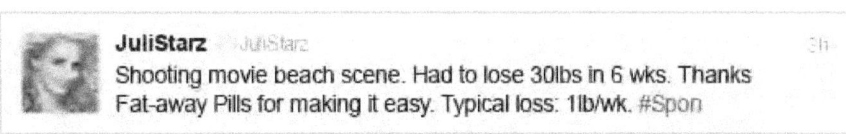

Consumers might not understand that "#spon" means that the message was sponsored by an advertiser. If a significant proportion of reasonable viewers would not, then the ad would be deceptive.

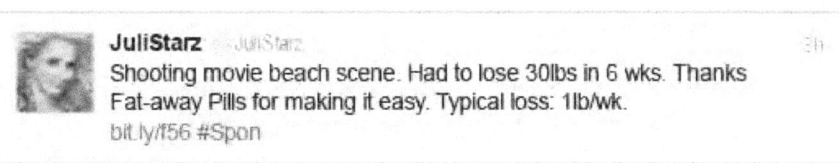

Putting #spon directly after the link might confuse consumers and make it less likely that they would understand that it is a disclosure.

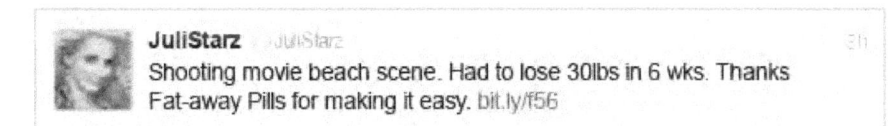

Consumers viewing "bit.ly/f56," which links to the advertiser's official website for the product, might not realize the nature and relevance of the information that could be found by clicking on it. Moreover, if consumers can buy Fat-away in brick and mortar stores, at third-party online retailers, or in any way other than by clicking on the link, consumers who do not click on the link would be misled.

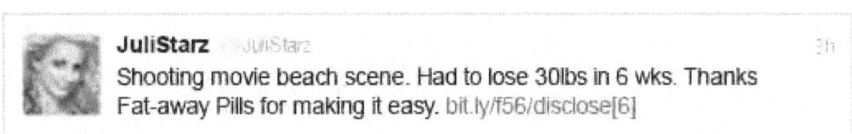

Similarly, consumers viewing "bit.ly/f56/disclose[6]," which leads to a third-party website with disclosures, would not necessarily understand what they will find at that website, or why they should click on that link.

Example 18

Both disclosures in this ad appear in text that contrasts poorly with the background of the page and they therefore are both easy to miss. Because the disclosures are not prominent, they are not clear and conspicuous.

Example 19

Most webpages viewable on desktop devices may also be viewable on smartphones, but, as discussed earlier, consumers may miss disclosures on mobile devices because of the need to zoom in on text and to scroll horizontally as well as vertically.

Disclosures are more likely to be clear and conspicuous on websites that are optimized for mobile devices or created using responsive design, which automatically detects the kind of device the consumer is using to access the site and arranges the content on the site so it makes sense for that device.

In this example, the website is optimized for mobile devices, and both the information about the service plan requirement and the hyperlink to the plan's prices are immediately adjacent to the camera price they qualify.

Example 20

Because the negative option in this example (enrollment in a recipe club) addresses a different subject than the main offer (cookware), the advertiser should take special care to ensure that the disclosure of the negative option is clear and conspicuous. In this case, requiring consumers to affirmatively acknowledge the disclosure by clicking on one of the two boxes on the second page — neither of which has been preselected — before they can proceed to checkout, should achieve that goal.

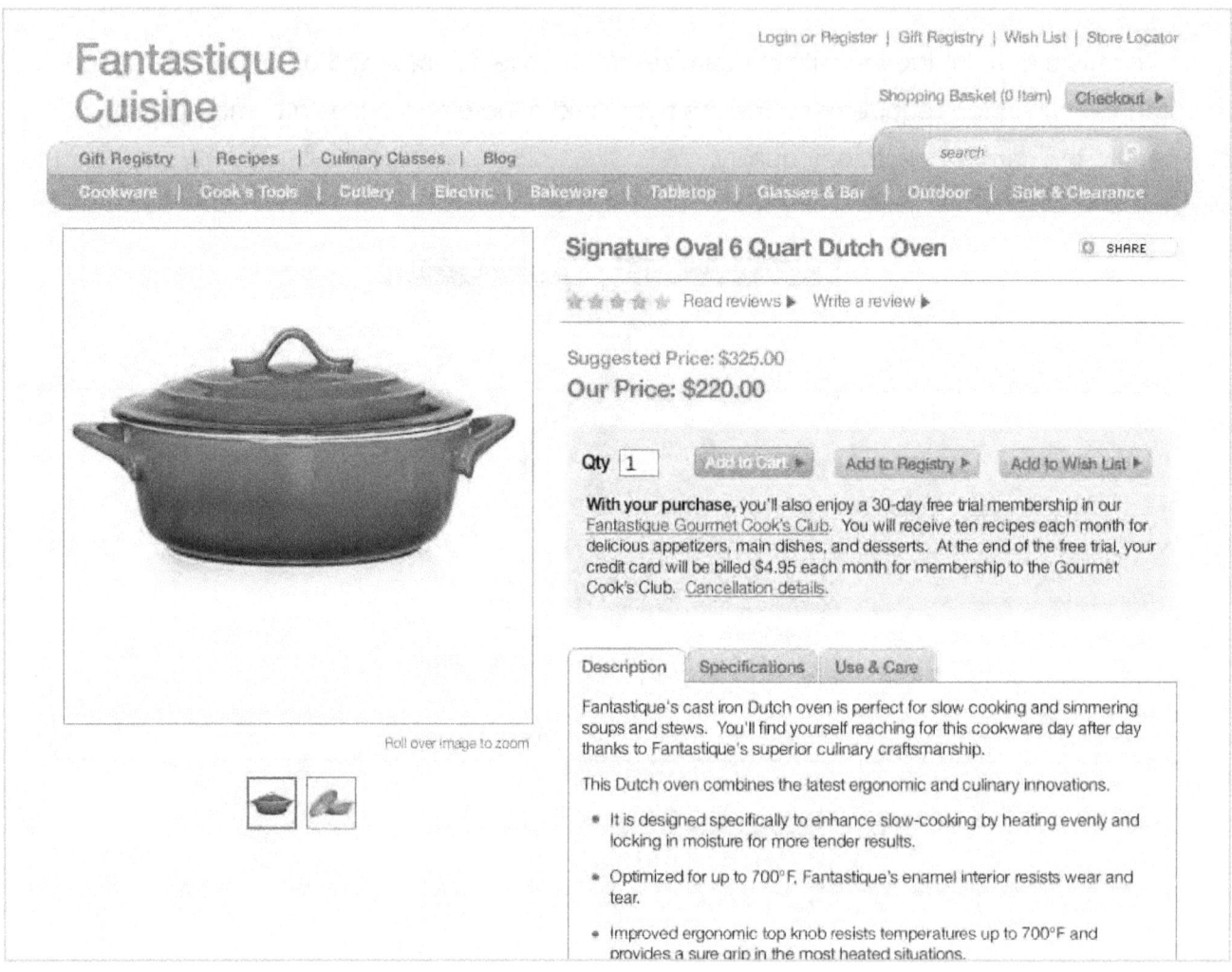

(continue on next page)

Example 20 (continued)

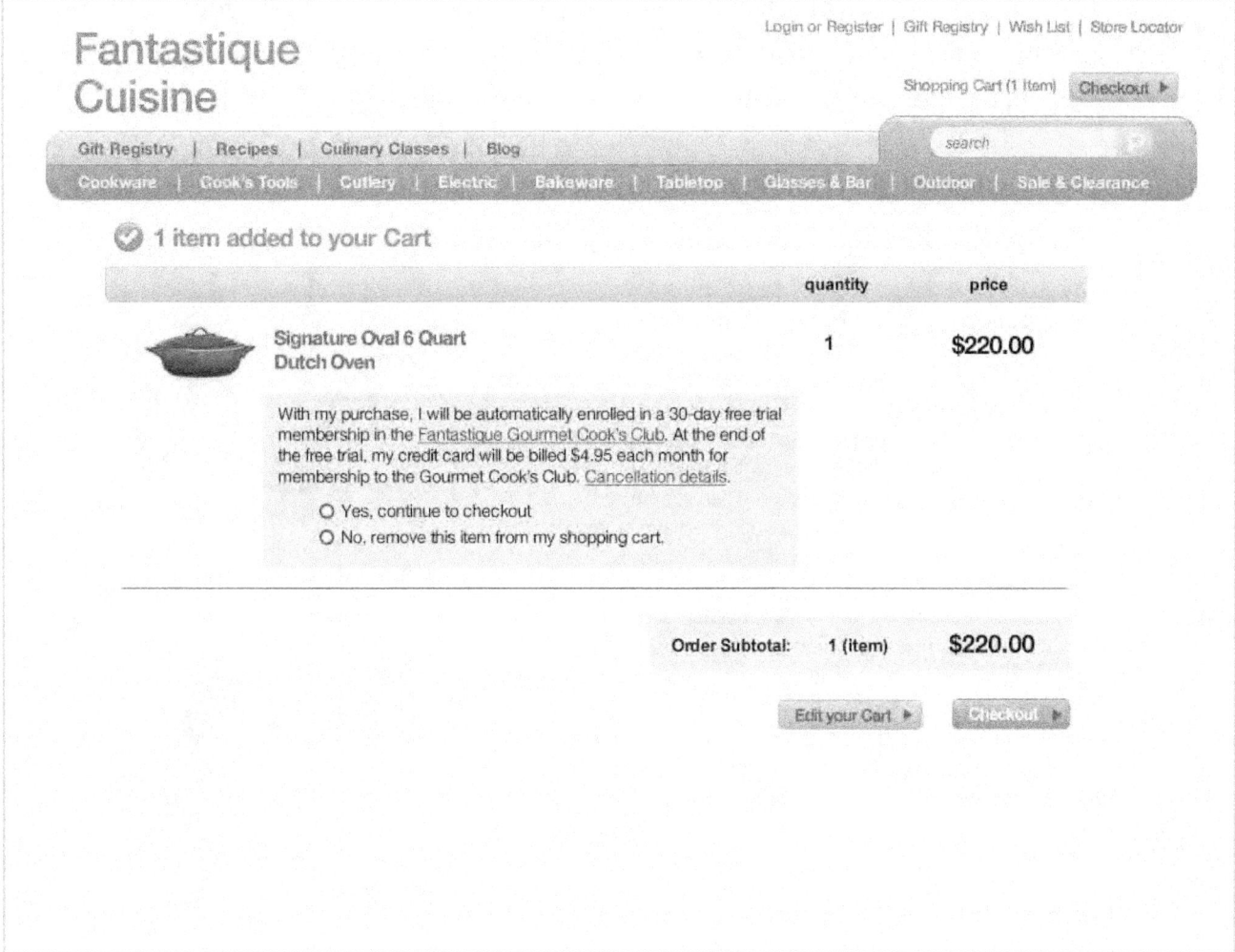

Example 21

The blogger in this example obtained the paint she is reviewing for free and must disclose that fact. Although she does so at the end of her blog post, there are several hyperlinks before that disclosure that could distract readers and cause them to click away before they get to the end of the post. Given these distractions, the disclosure likely is not clear and conspicuous.

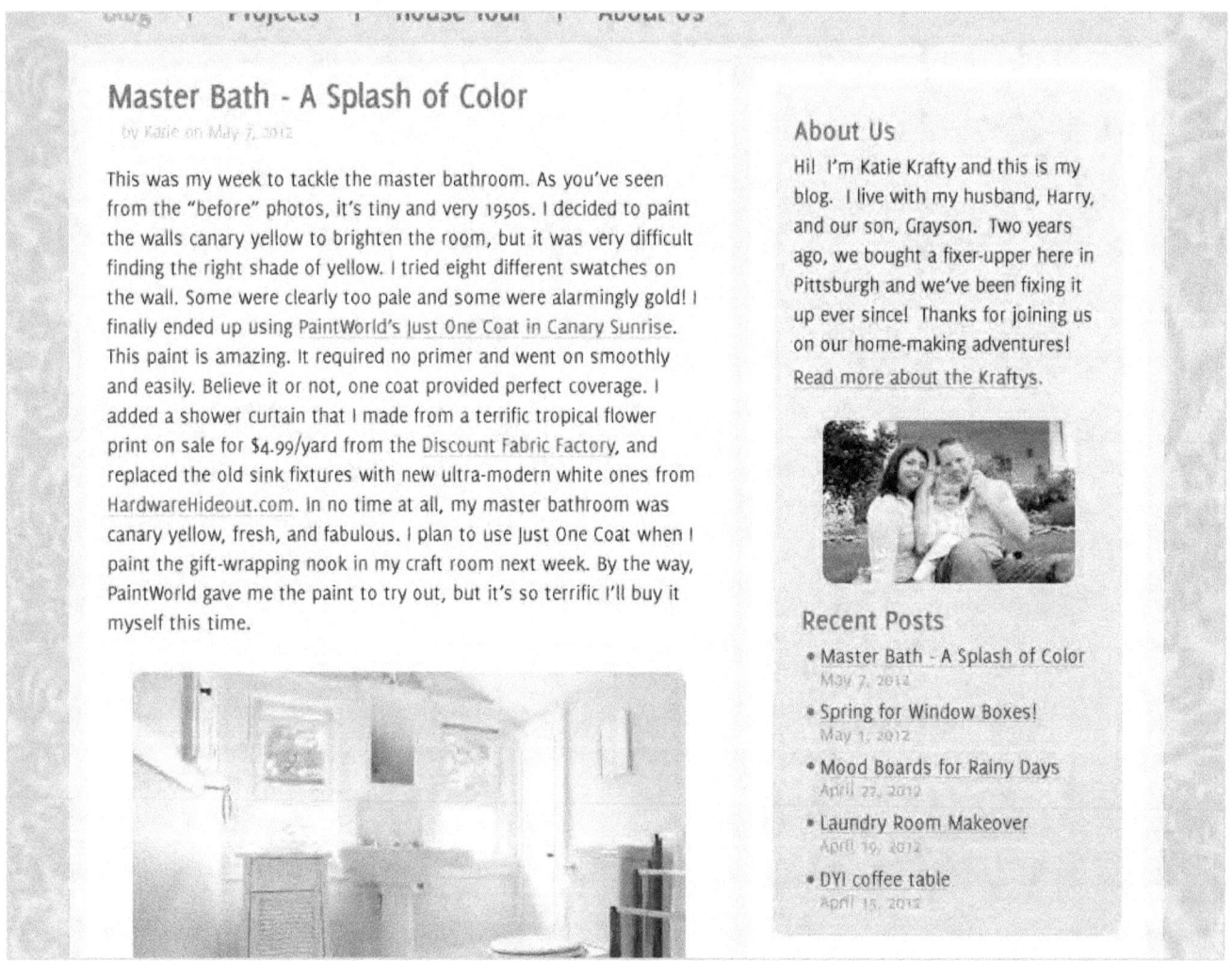

Blog | Projects | House Tour | About Us

Master Bath - A Splash of Color
by Katie on May 7, 2012

This was my week to tackle the master bathroom. As you've seen from the "before" photos, it's tiny and very 1950s. I decided to paint the walls canary yellow to brighten the room, but it was very difficult finding the right shade of yellow. I tried eight different swatches on the wall. Some were clearly too pale and some were alarmingly gold! I finally ended up using PaintWorld's Just One Coat in Canary Sunrise. This paint is amazing. It required no primer and went on smoothly and easily. Believe it or not, one coat provided perfect coverage. I added a shower curtain that I made from a terrific tropical flower print on sale for $4.99/yard from the Discount Fabric Factory, and replaced the old sink fixtures with new ultra-modern white ones from HardwareHideout.com. In no time at all, my master bathroom was canary yellow, fresh, and fabulous. I plan to use Just One Coat when I paint the gift-wrapping nook in my craft room next week. By the way, PaintWorld gave me the paint to try out, but it's so terrific I'll buy it myself this time.

About Us
Hi! I'm Katie Krafty and this is my blog. I live with my husband, Harry, and our son, Grayson. Two years ago, we bought a fixer-upper here in Pittsburgh and we've been fixing it up ever since! Thanks for joining us on our home-making adventures! Read more about the Kraftys.

Recent Posts
- Master Bath - A Splash of Color
  May 7, 2012
- Spring for Window Boxes!
  May 1, 2012
- Mood Boards for Rainy Days
  April 22, 2012
- Laundry Room Makeover
  April 19, 2012
- DYI coffee table
  April 15, 2012

Example 22

All of the elements of an ad should be considered in assessing whether a disclosure is clear and conspicuous. In some cases, elements that the advertiser might think make an ad more eye-catching could actually distract consumers from important disclosures.

In this example, an animated spokesperson moving around and discussing the benefits of the Eye on Your Home monitoring cameras might distract consumers from the disclosure of the monthly monitoring fee.